# HOW
# TO MAKE
# MONEY
# ONLINE

# Theory & Strategy

## The Ultimate Guide to Building Multiple Income Streams

# Table of contents

# Introduction

In today's fast-paced and ever-changing world, having a single source of income is no longer enough to secure a comfortable and fulfilling lifestyle. With the rise of the gig economy, remote work, and digital entrepreneurship, there are more opportunities than ever before to build multiple income streams and create a diversified and sustainable income portfolio.

Whether you're looking to earn extra income on the side, achieve financial freedom, or turn your passions into profitable businesses, The Ultimate Guide to Building Multiple Income Streams is the perfect resource to help you get started. This book is a comprehensive roadmap that covers everything from the fundamentals of passive income to building a successful online business, monetizing your skills and expertise, growing your wealth through smart investments, starting and scaling your own business, and much more.

With practical tips, real-life examples, and proven strategies, this guide will help you navigate the world of multiple income streams and achieve your financial goals. So whether you're a freelancer, an entrepreneur, an investor, or just someone looking to earn extra income, this book is the perfect tool to help you create a sustainable and diversified income portfolio that will provide you with financial security and peace of mind for years to come.

Diversifying income streams is essential for achieving financial stability and security for several reasons:

1. **Spreading financial risk:** Relying on a single source of income can be risky, especially in today's unpredictable economy. Diversifying income streams helps spread the risk of losing income due to job loss, economic downturns, or unexpected events.
2. **Increasing income potential:** By creating multiple streams of income, individuals can increase their earning potential and improve their overall financial health.
3. **Reducing dependence on one source of income:** Depending on a single source of income can create a sense of vulnerability, especially if that source is unstable or unreliable. Diversifying income streams can help reduce dependence on any one source of income and create a more stable financial situation.
4. **Providing flexibility:** Multiple streams of income can provide flexibility in terms of working hours and the ability to pursue different opportunities. This can create a more satisfying and fulfilling work-life balance.
5. **Creating a safety net:** Having multiple income streams can create a safety net in case of unexpected events, such as medical emergencies, natural disasters, or other financial emergencies.

Overall, diversifying income streams is a crucial aspect of achieving financial stability and security, providing individuals with more options, flexibility, and peace of mind.

## Overview of the book's key concepts

1. Diversifying income streams is important to increase financial security and stability.
2. Passive income streams offer benefits and can be generated both online and offline.
3. Building a successful online business involves identifying a niche, building an online presence, driving traffic, and maximizing revenue through online channels.
4. Freelancing and consulting offer opportunities to monetize skills and expertise, targeting potential clients, pricing services, and building a successful business.
5. Investing can grow wealth through profitable opportunities and building a diverse portfolio while minimizing risk.
6. Entrepreneurship involves identifying market opportunities, building a successful business from the ground up, and scaling and expanding over time.
7. Traditional business models involve buying wholesale and selling at a markup, identifying profitable products and services, and building a successful business through traditional channels.
8. The book provides strategies, tips, and techniques for building multiple income streams, both online and offline.

# Chapter 1

# The Fundamentals of Passive Income

## The benefits of passive income streams

Your money may expand, you may be able to retire earlier, you may be able to live the lifestyle of a digital nomad, and your riches may give you an alternate wealth choice. By developing several avenues via which you might generate passive income, you will reduce your reliance on any of them being successful.

**Passive income streams offer several benefits, including:**

**Reduced effort:** Unlike active income, which requires ongoing effort to maintain, passive income streams are generated with minimal effort once they are established.

## Freeing Up Your Time:

A passive income stream may enhance your quality of life in many ways, and this is one of the best. More downtime throughout the day is a great way to strike a better work-life balance. You'll feel like you have more control over your time, significantly reducing the stress you're under daily. You'll have more hours for self-care, pursuing passions, and meaningful time with loved ones. One might consider the extra time a chance to boost their earnings even further. Instead of stopping with just one passive income stream, why not create two or three? Maybe there's something you've always been curious about but felt you had the resources or stability to really pursue. Passive income streams can be generated from various sources, including investments, rental properties, online businesses, and other opportunities. This provides flexibility regarding income sources and the ability to generate income while pursuing other interests or activities.

**Reduced dependency on active income:** Passive income streams can minimize dependence on active income, providing a more stable and secure financial situation.

Scalability: Passive income streams can be scaled up or down depending on the desired income level and the amount of effort invested.

**Potential for long-term income:** Passive income streams can generate income over the long term, even after the initial investment or effort has been made.

## Improved Financial Security

Due to the ever-evolving nature of the market brought on by technological progress, formerly considered secure jobs are gradually disappearing. Nowadays, employees need to be more adaptable in their job search and choice of vocations. Yet, betting everything on passive income is becoming a riskier and more uncertain approach. That's why spreading your earnings over many streams is so smart: it reduces your overall exposure to risk while increasing your potential for profit. Earning money in a passive manner is a fantastic way to diversify your income and increase your chances of surviving financially in the event that you lose your primary source of income, such as a job. It may also be helpful if you're looking for strategies to beef up your funds for old age.

## More Control Over Your Work-Life

Your passive income stream should, by definition, need little upkeep beyond the initial setup phase. Likewise, you can arrange these commitments to meet your schedule and attend to them at your convenience. As a bonus, you can drum to your drum without leaving your house. With passive income, you can live anywhere you choose. And since everything can be arranged online, why not go abroad and learn about other cultures? It's also important to note that "passive" income is not always undemanding. Your plan is open to modification to accommodate your evolving needs. Yet, you should prepare yourself to revert to a more passive role.

### How to Choose the Right Strategy

The most important rule to remember while pursuing passive income is to stick to what you already know. Examine your capabilities and inventory the tools at your disposal.

It's not impossible to break into an area where you have no experience and find success. But , this strategy would need a great deal more work and carry more dangers, negating some of the primary advantages of passive income. You may double your passive income by repeating the steps you used to set up your first source of it. Incorporating new sources of income should be done methodically to avoid taking on more than you can or want to manage at once.

# Understanding the different types of passive income

Passive income is money earned from sources requiring little or no ongoing effort. Understanding the different types of passive income is essential for identifying opportunities to build multiple streams of income and generate wealth over the long term. Here's a more detailed explanation of each type of passive income:

**Rental income:** Rental income is generated by leasing out a property to tenants. Apartment buildings, workplaces, and retail establishments are all fair game here. Although rental income has the potential to generate a passive income stream, it does need an upfront investment in the property as well as continual management to keep it maintained and occupied.

**Investment income:** Investment income is generated from stocks, bonds, mutual funds, or other investments that generate passive income, such as dividends or interest payments. This type of passive income can provide a steady stream of income, but it also carries some level of risk and requires knowledge of investing to make informed investment decisions.

**Online business income:** Passive income can also be generated through an online business, such as affiliate marketing, online courses, or e-commerce sales. This can provide a flexible way to generate income from anywhere in the world, but it requires an initial investment of time and money to create and promote the business.

**Intellectual property income:** Royalties and licensing fees for intellectual property like patents, copyrights, or trademarks are the sources of this form of passive income. This can include income from books, music, or other creative works. Intellectual property income can provide a steady stream of income, but it requires creativity and the ability to create valuable intellectual property that others are willing to pay for.

**Real estate crowdfunding:** Crowdfunding platforms can provide opportunities for passive income through real estate investments. This involves pooling funds with other investors to invest in real estate projects, such as apartment buildings, commercial properties, or land development. This can provide a way to invest in real estate without the need for significant capital, but it carries some level of risk and requires knowledge of real estate investing.

**Peer-to-peer lending:** This involves lending money to others through peer-to-peer lending platforms, which can generate interest income. This can provide a way to earn higher interest rates than traditional savings accounts or CDs, but it carries some level of risk and requires knowledge of lending and credit risk.

**Business ownership:** Passive income can be generated through business ownership, such as owning rental properties, investing in a business, or owning stocks in a company. This can provide a way to create passive income while also benefiting from the potential growth and profits of the business.

**Network marketing:** This involves generating passive income by building a network of distributors or salespeople who generate sales and commissions. This can provide a flexible way to generate revenue from anywhere in the world, but it requires an initial investment of time and effort to build a network and generate sales.

Overall, understanding the different types of passive income is essential for identifying the best opportunities for generating passive income and building a diversified income portfolio. It is necessary to evaluate each kind of passive income based on its potential returns, the level of effort required, and the risks involved.

## Tips for generating passive income online and offline

Passive income may be generated online and offline, and it is a fantastic method to make money with little to no work. Investing in real estate to collect rent is a common passive income strategy. This may be accomplished in a variety of ways, including direct investments in real estate, such as the purchase and rental of a property, or indirectly via participation in real estate crowdfunding initiatives. Passive investment income may also be generated by purchasing dividend-paying equities or mutual funds. Another way to make money online without doing anything is to make digital items like e-books or online courses. Royalties from licensing your patent or trademark might be another source of passive income. The interest earned via peer-to-peer lending is a relatively recent approach that may be passively maintained. Successful blogging or website development may generate residual earnings from advertising and affiliate programs. Last but not least, offline businesses may generate revenue by selling tangible goods or services like those offered by a tutoring service or a craft shop. To ensure your financial security and success, you need to investigate your options and diversify your income sources before settling on the right course for you.

# Chapter 2

# Building a Successful Online Business

## Identifying a market niche

Identifying a market niche is essential for building a successful online business. A market niche is a specific subset of a larger market with particular needs or preferences. By identifying a market niche, you can create a product or service that specifically meets the needs of that niche, which can help differentiate your business from others in the market and make it easier to target potential customers. To identify a market niche, you need to conduct market research. This involves gathering information about the larger market, including demographics, buying habits, and preferences. Having thoroughly comprehended the market, you can now zero in on certain segments with unmet wants or preferences. This can involve looking for gaps in the market or areas with a high level of competition but a low level of differentiation. It's important to choose a niche you are interested in and know about. This will help you to create a product or service that is not only profitable but also something you enjoy working on. Additionally, you should also consider the size of the niche. If the niche is too small, you may not be able to generate enough revenue to sustain your business. On the other hand, if the niche is too broad, you may have difficulty differentiating your business from others in the market. Once you have identified a market niche, you can create a product or service that specifically meets the needs of that niche. This can involve tailoring your product or service to specific customer needs or preferences or creating a unique product or service that fills a market gap. By focusing on a specific market niche and creating a product or service that meets the needs of that niche, you can create a more successful online business that is more likely to attract and retain customers.

## Strategies for building an online presence

Creating a solid online identity is a must if you want to launch a profitable online company. When you have a solid online presence, you boost your company's reputation and the number of people who can see your advertisements.

Methods to increase your visibility online include the following:

**Create a professional website:** Establishing credibility in the digital world begins with a polished website. Your website's design, functionality, and content should all reflect well on your company. Your website needs search engine optimization so that people looking for items or services like yours may find it.

## Utilize social media:

Promoting your content on Facebook, Twitter, and Instagram can increase brand awareness and engagement. Your social media approach should include publishing, connecting with followers, and sponsored advertising.

**Develop content:** High-quality content may promote reputation and revenue. Content strategies should contain blogs, videos, infographics, and other valuable information.

**Engage with your audience:** Having conversations with your target demographic is crucial to expanding your online visibility. Quick and competent replies to messages, comments, and reviews are expected. As a result, your consumers will see that you care about them and appreciate their business.

**Utilize email marketing:** Email marketing is a great method to contact current and future clients. A regular email newsletter, promotions, and other useful information should be part of your email marketing plan.

By following these tactics, you may boost your company's reputation and client base and your exposure to new consumers and income.

# Techniques for driving traffic and generating leads

Every online company must attract visitors to their site and turn them into leads. A few methods to increase exposure and potential clients are as follows:

## Search engine optimization (SEO):

Search engine optimization (SEO) enhances a website's visibility in organic search results. To do this, you need to do keyword research, tweak your website's content and layout, and construct credible inbound connections.

## Pay-per-click (PPC) advertising:

Using pay-per-click (PPC) advertising, your adverts will appear on search engine results pages and other websites. Pay-per-click advertising is a smart strategy for attracting qualified visitors to your site since you just have to cover the costs associated with actual clicks.

## Social media advertising:

Ads on social media sites like Facebook, Instagram, and Twitter may be tailored to a particular audience based on their demographics and interests. Such an approach may be useful for attracting new visitors to your site and securing new business.

## Content marketing:

To use content marketing, you must provide material that informs or entertains your intended audience. This may be in the form of blog articles, movies, infographics, or anything else that can be written or visually presented. Offering value to your intended audience increases the likelihood of them becoming paying customers.

## Email marketing:

Email marketing is an effective strategy for maintaining relationships with current and new clients. Email marketing is a powerful tool for promoting your business's goods and services, sharing useful information with your target market, and attracting potential customers.With these methods, you may increase qualified visitors to your site, which can increase your chances of making a sale and hence your income.

## Add Social Sharing Buttons to Your Website:

Getting people to talk about your business and products on social media is the holy grail of contemporary marketing. The more social sharing icons you have on your site, the simpler it will be for your viewers to spread your material to their networks. Most modern website themes have social media share buttons as standard, and many free and premium plugins are also available.

## Paid Search:

Even if you find a lot of success using free methods, you may still want to invest in some paid advertising. In reality, purchased traffic is self-funding if your website is converting successfully. In today's market, paid search advertising like Google AdWords is one of the easiest ways to get shoppers to your website.

## Build Connections in Your Niche:

I know it's a cliche, but networking with other industry insiders may lead to natural backlinks and more referral traffic. Even though almost all of the most effective marketers already do this, the vast majority of marketers still don't.

## Make Sure Your Site is Responsive:

You need to have a mobile-friendly site today. A responsive design won't increase your site's traffic, but a non-responsive design will decrease it. Most internet users now access the web through mobile devices, and those who visit a site that isn't mobile-friendly are less likely to spend time there.

## Tips for maximizing revenue through online channels

Today's businesses need a strong internet presence. Online income maximization is crucial to online company success.

One key tip for maximizing revenue through online channels is to offer multiple payment options. By providing customers with various payment options, such as credit cards, PayPal, and Apple Pay, you can increase the likelihood of a successful transaction and reduce cart abandonment rates. Another effective strategy for maximizing revenue is to use pricing strategies. This could include bundling products or services, offering tiered pricing based on the level of service, or providing limited-time discounts. These strategies can encourage customers to make a purchase and increase the average order value.

Upselling and cross-selling are additional tactics that can be used to increase revenue through online channels. During the checkout process, offering complementary products or services can encourage customers to purchase additional items. By making it easy and convenient for customers to add related products to their orders, you can increase the total value of each transaction.

There are several strategies for identifying and capitalizing on profitable online business opportunities:

Examine the market and identify any shifts or openings. Find out what people want most, then figure out how to provide it to them. Make connections with other business owners and professionals in your field to share ideas and learn from each other's successes and failures. Experiment with several approaches to your company to find the ones that provide the greatest results. Spread your bets, and don't risk everything on one venture. Diversifying your bets among a number of projects helps you spread out your risk.

Implementing retargeting campaigns is another effective way to maximize revenue through online channels. Retargeting displays adverts to website visitors who did not buy. This can help bring them back to your website and encourage them to make a purchase.

Finally, optimizing your website for conversions can significantly increase revenue through online channels. This involves creating a simple and intuitive checkout process, providing social proof like customer reviews and testimonials, and using clear calls to action. Optimizing your website to encourage customers to take action can increase the conversion rate and maximize revenue through online channels.

Overall, there are many effective strategies for maximizing revenue through online channels, including offering multiple payment options, pricing strategies, upselling and cross-selling, implementing retargeting campaigns, and optimizing your website for conversions. By implementing these tactics effectively, you can increase the profitability of your online business and build a strong, sustainable source of passive income.

# Chapter 3

# Freelancing and Consulting: Monetizing Your Skills and Expertise

## Understanding the market for freelance and consulting services

The market for freelance and consulting services is growing, with more and more businesses turning to independent contractors for specialized services. Freelancing and consulting can offer a flexible and rewarding career path, allowing professionals to leverage their skills and expertise to provide high-quality services to clients in a variety of industries.

One of the first steps in understanding the market for freelance and consulting services is to research the industry and identify the target market. This involves analyzing market trends and identifying areas of demand for specific services. For example, web development, content creation, and digital marketing are all in high demand in today's digital economy. By identifying these areas of demand, freelancers and consultants can tailor their services to meet the needs of potential clients.

In addition to researching the market, it's important to identify the skills and expertise you can offer as a freelancer or consultant. This may involve evaluating your education, training, work experience, and other qualifications to identify areas of specialization. Once you have identified your areas of expertise, you can create a marketing strategy to promote your services and attract potential clients. This may include developing a website, creating marketing materials, and leveraging social media and other platforms to build your online presence and establish your brand.

Pricing your services is another important aspect of understanding the market for freelance and consulting services. This involves researching industry rates and evaluating your qualifications and experience when setting prices. It's important to establish a pricing strategy that balances competitiveness with profitability. While it may be tempting to price your services low in order to attract clients, it's important to remember that your time and expertise have value. By setting fair and competitive rates, you can build a sustainable and profitable freelance or consulting business.

Networking and building relationships with potential clients is also a key part of understanding the freelance and consulting services market. This involves attending industry events, connecting with other professionals in your field, and leveraging online platforms to connect with potential clients. You may acquire high-quality customers and develop a reputation for excellent services by creating a strong network and becoming an expert in your sector.

Understanding the freelance and consulting services market is essential for building a successful and profitable business. By researching the industry, identifying your areas of expertise, pricing your services competitively, and building a strong network, you can establish yourself as a leader in your field and generate multiple income streams.

## Strategies for identifying and targeting potential clients

Freelance and consulting service providers might find new customers via research and networking. Knowing who you're selling to and what problems they're trying to solve is crucial before you can provide any help. You might begin by locating prospective customers using social media, professional networking sites, and online job boards. When reaching out to prospective customers, it's crucial to do it in a manner that's both personable and relevant to the requirements you know you'll be meeting. To do so, you may need to create a persuasive pitch that shows your qualifications and explains how you can assist the company in meeting its objectives. You may use your current network to your advantage by requesting references and recommendations from satisfied customers and business associates.

Creating a name for oneself in your profession as an authority figure is also crucial. Building a professional online presence might include having an active social media profile and a website where you regularly publish information demonstrating your expertise. You may win over new customers and expand your network by building credibility and visibility online. Researching the competition and spotting holes in the market is another crucial tactic for locating and attracting new customers in the freelancing and consulting service sectors. You may distinguish yourself as a unique and valued solution that solves unmet requirements by studying your sector's competitive environment and the services already being supplied.

Data-driven methods like search engine optimization (SEO) and pay-per-click (PPC) advertising may also help you get your name out there and in front of prospective customers. You may boost your organic traffic and visibility in SERPs by optimizing your website and content for relevant keywords. In addition, pay-per-click (PPC) advertising lets you zero in on certain keywords and demographics, boosting your exposure to customers looking for services like yours. Finally, constant client contact and excellent service are essential. Customer satisfaction increases the likelihood of referrals and positive evaluations. You may become a dependable partner in your customers' businesses' success if you regularly provide them with value and cultivate solid connections with them.

## Tips for pricing your services and maximizing revenue

Knowing your financial objectives before deciding how much to charge for your goods is crucial. Increasing profits is a common goal for many businesses. Others may make alterations to their works to increase brand recognition. Offering discounts might entice potential buyers to try a product for the first time. While this pricing strategy may harm a product's short-term profitability, it might help bring in new consumers who are more likely to buy other products, some of which may have greater profit margins.To attract new consumers, a business can, for instance, provide the product or service at a discounted rate during a trial period. As the trial ends, some consumers may decide to keep their memberships, while others may cancel. As a result, this may aid the business in reaching its financial objectives. Talking to managers, supervisors, or executives about the company's financial objectives is a good first step. When pricing your freelance or consulting services, it's important to consider various factors to ensure that you are both competitive and profitable. Here are some tips for pricing your services and maximizing revenue:

**Determine your hourly rate or project fee:** Calculate your desired income and the number of hours or projects you can realistically take on in a given period. This will give you a baseline hourly rate or project fee that you can use to price your services.

**Research the market:** Look at what other freelancers or consultants in your industry charge for similar services. Knowing the current market pricing might help you price your services competitively.

**Consider your experience and expertise:** If you have specialized skills or extensive experience in a certain area, you may be able to charge a higher rate than someone just starting.

**Account for expenses:** Don't forget to factor in expenses such as taxes, software subscriptions, equipment, and other costs when pricing your services.

**Offer tiered pricing:** Consider offering different service packages at different price points to appeal to a wider range of clients and increase revenue.

**Upsell and cross-sell:** Look for opportunities to upsell or cross-sell additional services to existing clients. For example, if you're a graphic designer, you could offer to design a client's business cards in addition to their website.

**Establish value-based pricing:** Rather than charging by the hour or project, you could consider value-based pricing, which considers your services' value to the client. For example, this could involve charging a percentage of your work's revenue to the client.

By considering these factors and developing a comprehensive pricing strategy, you can maximize your revenue and ensure your services are priced competitively and profitably.

# Techniques for building a successful freelance and consulting business

There is more to running a successful freelancing or consulting firm than doing excellent work. To succeed, you must create a memorable brand, foster meaningful connections with customers, and successfully sell your services. Concentrating on a single market or field might help freelancers and consultants succeed. Having a robust internet presence is another strategy. Creating a blog or other content marketing with a good website and social media accounts may help spread the word about your work and skills. Building rapport and expanding your clientele by networking with other experts in your field. Furthermore, ensure you have a method for keeping in touch with customers and handling your task. Some examples of this include employing project management software to keep organized and in constant communication with customers on the status of their projects. It takes time and effort to start a successful freelancing and consulting company. Still, if you invest in creating a memorable brand, networking, and promoting yourself, you can bring in new customers and grow your business.

## Qualities needed for successful freelancing

A successful independent contractor will have a healthy mix of talent, interest, and motivation to make money. Enjoyment of the screen industry and its products. The knowledge required to contribute to the content creation. Economic motivation to make a life in the field. The motivation to make money is essential since, without it, you have a pastime. Your need for cash compels you to pursue a career in this field.

## Motivation and discipline

The best freelancers are self-driven and can set and stick to strict deadlines. They keep their clientele up to date promptly. They are aware of whether or not they can handle more responsibilities or if they should suggest a coworker instead. Keeping yourself motivated while in a hectic production is simple, but it's far more challenging when you're between contracts and need to find new work or organize your money. If you aren't naturally self-disciplined, Maintaining your duties requires work. Likewise, even the most disciplined individuals sometimes need to work on doing what they perceive to be the least appealing work.

## Reputation

Professionalism and reputation are crucial because people will judge you based on the work you did for them in the past. Due to the lack of a corporate shield, freelancers must face their customers directly while providing services. If you want to go forward, you should treat your good name like gold. In the form of recommendations from coworkers and customers, it always shows up before you do. The job in this industry is strenuous because of the long hours and frequent travel required. Having a positive reputation as someone easy to get along with is crucial.

**Flexibility**

Freelancers require flexibility and the ability to adapt to new circumstances. Companies and their customer bases evolve, necessitating a regular re-evaluation of services. Moreover, every single work is unique in its way. The more customers you work with, the more you'll realize that seemingly similar tasks may vary widely based on the nature of the client's business.

The other side of having a lot of room for maneuvering is having to click with a customer and their team immediately so you can start working. Both of you know about the other's life and what may be happening. When everyone works hard for a limited time, there is little motivation to invest in building long-term working relationships; instead, the emphasis should be on getting the task done. This implies that those who work for themselves often need clarification on whether or not they are meeting their client's expectations. Hence, they overachieve in pay to guarantee they accomplish their best job, which may cause stress and worry. These concerns may be greatly reduced if you can find methods to actively include the customer in providing periodic feedback on your work.

**Sector knowledge**

Just having an interest in working in the field is not enough. You need to have a strong grasp of the position you're applying for, along with a genuine interest in and perspective on the work being done in that field. No matter what field you're now in or want to enter, an understanding of and comfort in talking about the various content realization processes is essential. It includes not only the plots but also the visuals, audio, and gameplay.

# Chapter 4

# Investing: Growing Your Wealth Through Smart Investments

## Understanding the basics of investing

In economic terms, "wealth" refers to a surplus of funds, while "wealth creation" is the process of generating such a surplus. When our debts, such mortgages and car payments, are subtracted from our assets, such as houses, cash, gold, stocks, and mutual fund shares, we arrive at our net worth. Yet, prosperity is a relative concept. Whether or whether one is affluent is according to one's own aspirational standard. If you have enough money to do everything you've ever wanted to do, then you may call yourself affluent.

The term "wealth creation" is used to describe the process of putting your savings to work in order to achieve your financial objectives. Achieving enough wealth development requires not only picking the proper investment but also giving it enough time to expand. You should start saving and investing as soon as you can so that you may get the most advantage from compounding. Those who begin investing at a young age have a greater chance of keeping their money in the market for a longer period of time, which may help them achieve a wider range of monetary objectives. Increasing your investment in proportion to your income growth is another approach to guarantee you reach your wealth building target. An yearly raise is something you may expect if you get a salary. You may save a lot more money if you raise your monthly investments by the same amount every year as your yearly increment. When first getting started in the world of investing, the amount you put in is more important than the rate of return you get.

There is no one certain technique to amass riches, since everyone has different goals and time horizons. Long-term investors, for instance, would be better served by equity-oriented investments than debt-oriented ones. Debt and Hybrid Mutual Funds, on the other hand, are better suited to short- and medium-term objectives. Creating wealth entails, at its core, expanding one's money in order to meet numerous short-, intermediate-, and long-term monetary objectives. Saving for a trip or a new iPhone might be examples of short-term financial objectives. This category includes objectives with a time frame of three years or fewer. For most people, three to five years is a reasonable time frame to focus on when setting and achieving medium-term objectives related to investments. Saving for a new automobile, saving for a down payment on a home, etc., are all examples of wealth generation objectives. But, an investing horizon of many years or even decades is quite reasonable for saving enough for retirement or other similarly far-off objectives. If this is the case, you'll want to save up enough money while you're working to cover your expenses after you retire. Considering since there might be many wealth building goals with varying time horizons, you'll need to use a variety of tactics.

Investing is placing money into an asset or financial instrument with the expectation of future gain. If you want to amass riches and ensure your financial stability, you must learn the fundamentals of investing. The first step in investing is deciding how much money you are ready to risk and establishing concrete financial objectives. While investing, it's crucial to evaluate your risk tolerance or the amount of uncertainty you're ready to accept in exchange for a potential reward. Stocks, bonds, mutual funds, exchange-traded funds (ETFs), and real estate are some of the many investment options available. To make the most informed investment decision, you should familiarize yourself with the nuances of each of them before committing money. One of the most important investment strategies is diversifying your investments. So, you limit the danger of losing too much in a market slump and diversify your assets. Investors must also consider the costs associated with their assets. The likes of commissions, management fees, and other costs may drastically cut your profits. Last but not least, make sure you're aware of how your assets are doing and the larger economic and market situations that may have an impact. If you want to ensure you're on pace to reach your financial objectives, keeping tabs on your investments and making any required modifications regularly is important.

## Strategies for identifying profitable investment opportunities

Every one of us is familiar with the tenet of sound investing: Buy cheap, sell high. Yet, putting this adage into practice may be challenging, particularly if your friends and coworkers are not following it. These methods can aid you in finding profitable investment opportunities:

The time to buy is now. Find out what an investment or purchase should be worth at a minimum and wait to acquire it until the price drops below that level. It is best to search for purchasing opportunities when the stock market collapses, and individuals are selling out of fear. You want to buy an asset after it has dropped in price greatly because you believe it will eventually increase in value and provide a profit.The time to sell is now. It's best to think about selling an item when its value has increased significantly. This is typical of a rising market when many investors are looking to make purchases. Significant gains in an investment signal the right moment to take profits. You might put the money into a more secure investment, or you could try your luck with another underperforming asset.

Observe and get knowledge from the bad weather. One's best efforts to purchase cheap and sell high will inevitably result in some losses. Investing with the hope of making a profit would be common practice if it were simple. Whenever you experience a loss on an investment, it's important not to let it cause you to lose sleep or to stop investing entirely. Maybe you're ready to take a vacation from active investing and let an index fund help you reap the rewards of the market. Alternately, you can see the importance of doing one's homework before risking more money than one can afford to lose on an investment. Let fear not hold you back from reaching your full potential. Instead, use the strength you gained from enduring adversity as the impetus for future accomplishments.

Fear may be a useful tool for self-evaluation. Analyze the returns on your previous investments and consider how they might be improved in the future. Physically writing out consequences you want to avoid is a great way to get understanding. An investing strategy in writing might help you avoid making rash choices while your emotions are running high. Having a trusted third party, such as a financial advisor, tax consultant, or legal advisor, review your investment proposals may offer an extra degree of trustworthiness and responsibility.

If you want to prevent looking back with regret, make a plan. Regret over a poor investment choice is understandable after suffering a significant loss. Nevertheless, there's also the remorse of missing out on a lucrative investment opportunity at the bottom level. You may minimize the possibility of a bad outcome by first making a list of your investment choices and then carefully considering each one. Having anything written down will help you stay on track when you're feeling tempted by friends or experts. If you want to take it a step further, you can also assess your life priorities and the ways in which your money may help you reach them via the planning process.

The ultimate goal of investing should be to provide for one's preferred way of life. If you make the right decisions, you may amass enough money to retire early or quit your miserable work. To amass riches, though, you'll need to use sound reasoning and be steadfast in your financial strategy. Financial success is unlikely to be attained by blindly following the newest investing fad. Every one of us is familiar with the tenet of sound investing: Buy cheap, sell high. Yet, putting this adage into practice may be challenging, particularly if your friends and coworkers are not following it. These methods can aid you in finding profitable investment opportunities:

**Buy low:** Find out what an investment or purchase should be worth at a minimum and wait to acquire it until the price drops below that level. It is best to search for purchasing opportunities when the stock market collapses, and individuals are selling out of fear. You want to buy an asset after it has dropped in price greatly because you believe it will eventually increase in value and provide a profit.

## Sell high:

It's best to think about selling an item when its value has increased significantly. This is typical of a rising market when many investors are looking to make purchases. Significant gains in an investment signal the right moment to take profits. You might put the money into a more secure investment, or you could try your luck with another underperforming asset.

**Learn from the storms**: One's best efforts to purchase cheap and sell high will inevitably result in some losses. Investing with the hope of making a profit would be common practice if it were simple. Whenever you experience a loss on an investment, it's important not to let it cause you to lose sleep or to stop investing entirely. Maybe you're ready to take a vacation from active investing and let an index fund help you reap the rewards of the market. Alternately, you can see the importance of doing one's homework before risking more money than one can afford to lose on an investment. Let fear not hold you back from reaching your full potential. Instead, use the strength you gained from enduring adversity as the impetus for future accomplishments.

### Use your fear to self-assess:

Analyze the returns on your previous investments and consider how they might be improved in the future. Physically writing out consequences you want to avoid is a great way to get understanding. An investing strategy in writing might help you avoid making rash choices while your emotions are running high. Having a trusted third party, such as a financial advisor, tax consultant, or legal advisor, review your investment proposals may offer an extra degree of trustworthiness and responsibility.

### Create a plan to avoid regret.

Regret over a poor investment choice is understandable after suffering a significant loss. Nevertheless, there's also the remorse of missing out on a lucrative investment opportunity at the bottom level. You may minimize the possibility of a bad outcome by first making a list of your investment choices and then carefully considering each one. Having anything written down will help you stay on track when you're feeling tempted by friends or experts. If you want to take it a step further, you can also assess your life priorities and the ways in which your money may help you reach them via the planning process. The ultimate goal of investing should be to provide for one's preferred way of life. If you make the right decisions, you may amass enough money to retire early or quit your miserable work. To amass riches, though, you'll need to use sound reasoning and be steadfast in your financial strategy. Financial success is unlikely to be attained by blindly following the newest investing fad.

# Tips for minimizing risk and maximizing returns

To maximize profits, you should get the best potential return on your investment (ROI). Many methods exist for doing this:

Putting your money into equities with a strong growth rate might pay you handsomely in the long run. Stocks that pay dividends: If you're an investor who wants to maximize their profits, dividend stocks are a good bet since they often beat the market over time. A fantastic strategy to increase your long-term gains is to reinvest your dividends. You may accelerate your progress towards your financial objectives by using dividend reinvestment as a pay rise. One of the easiest methods to optimize your profits is to just stick to your various assets for the long term. Allowing them to compound and expand over time may result in substantial profits. Diversification is crucial for investors. Diversifying your investments across a number of asset types will help cushion the blow of a decline in value in any one area.

Investing using dollar-cost-averaging may help spread out your investment risk over time. Regular, predetermined investments help you ride out market fluctuations and avoid overpaying at peak times. Investing in index funds provides a convenient and efficient strategy for achieving portfolio diversification. You may potentially increase your profits by investing in an index fund since it will expose you to a large number of companies. When it comes to diversifying your portfolio, exchange-traded funds (ETFs) are a straightforward and efficient option. Investing in exchange-traded funds (ETFs) that follow a broad range of indices may help you maximize your returns. To increase profits, leverage might be used. Investing with borrowed funds raises the stakes in terms of possible returns (or losses). The danger of financial loss may be increased by using leverage inappropriately. Using a methodical approach to investment: The key to long-term success is a methodical approach. You'll have a better chance of success if you commit to your strategy and refrain from making impulsive choices.

**Learn to reduce investment risk and maximize returns via strategic diversification.**

Diversification is essential for lowering risk. Spreading your money across many investments helps you minimize loss. Diversification may be achieved in a few distinct ways. Spreading your money around across equities, bonds, and cash is one option. Diversifying one's investment portfolio across industries, including healthcare, technology, and consumer goods, is yet another option. Lastly, you may diversify your portfolio by investing in firms located in other nations. The optimal method of diversification is contextualized by the specifics of your situation and aims. Whether you choose to implement it, diversity is a crucial step in reducing your exposure to risk and safeguarding your investment portfolio. Diversification is essential for lowering risk. Spreading your money across many investments helps you minimize loss. To lower your investment's potential for loss, you may do one of two important things:

**Put your money in as many different places as possible.**

Invest in several things rather than depending on one. Diversify your portfolio among a variety of asset types and industries to lower your exposure to risk.

**Maintain a routine of reviewing your financial portfolio.**

Check-in on the progress of your portfolio and make adjustments as necessary. You may use this to keep on track and not take any unnecessary risks.

**Maintain your investing discipline.**

Don't allow your feelings to influence your judgment. Don't let short-term market swings cause you to abandon your strategy. If you stick to these guidelines, you should be able to keep your portfolio on track while reducing the potential for loss.

# Techniques for building a diverse investment portfolio

Complementarity is the foundation of portfolio diversity, and it refers to the degree to which two or more assets behave in opposing ways in certain contexts. No matter the individual risk profiles of the assets in a portfolio, that portfolio's overall risk may be reduced by choosing investments with a high degree of complementarity. Let's say you run a portfolio and decide to put money into two equities, which we'll refer to as Investment A and Investment B. A is invested in a parcel delivery service and B in a web conferencing service. The fact that the two assets are not in a closely linked industry reduces the portfolio's total risk, even though both are very dangerous. Investment A's stock price may fall if, for example, a gas shortage prevents the business from delivering deliveries. But, the value of Investment B might rise if investors realize that a gas shortage won't affect videoconferencing. Investment B's success may be inversely connected to Investment A's if the gas crisis prompts some individuals to work from home, leading them to invest in the videoconferencing platform. By investing in a variety of different vehicles, you may reduce your exposure to any one loss.

A diversified investment portfolio is the result of the following steps:

- Assess your risk tolerance before starting a portfolio. Depending on factors including your age, life circumstances, and level of investing expertise, you may have a different level of comfort with risk.
- After you have established your comfort level with risk, you may go on to defining your investing objectives. Do you want to make money, amass wealth over time, or realize a specific financial goal, such as retirement or the college education of a child?
- Set your asset allocation: "asset allocation" describes the distribution of your investment capital among various asset types. Your asset allocation should reflect your willingness to take on risk and your long-term financial objectives.
- Choose specific assets within each asset class after your asset allocation has been established. You may, for instance, diversify the equity element of your

portfolio by including both domestic and foreign equities of varying market capitalizations. You may diversify your bond holdings by investing in a combination of government, corporate, and high-yield bonds.

- Lastly, it is crucial to keep an eye on your portfolio and rebalance it when necessary. To do this, you should check in on your asset allocation regularly and make any required modifications to align with your long-term investing objectives and comfort level with risk. To rebalance your portfolio, you may, for instance, sell some assets in a high-performing asset class and put the money towards purchases in a lower-performing asset class.

# Chapter 5

# Entrepreneurship: Starting and Scaling Your Own Business

## Understanding the fundamentals of entrepreneurship

Being the entrepreneur of a rapidly expanding company, business persons often see other entrepreneurs who have brilliant ideas but are unsure of how to turn those ideas into a sustainable business model. If you're fortunate, you may sell your website or app following a sudden influx of users and publicity. Most businesses, however, need intensive preparation, a distinct market niche, and a well-thought-out strategy for success. Upon starting business, entrepreneur zeroed in on a sizable market and discovered a lucrative and desirable niche.

Here's what I'd tell you if you wanted to start a business:

## Maintain reasonable expectations.

Although optimism and trust are essential in business planning, they should be tempered with a healthy dose of reality. Be realistic in your business predictions to save yourself and your company partners from being disappointed. Think about the company's size and industry before proceeding. Do you have a low-margin product that needs time to build traction? Or are you gambling with an app that might be a flop but could also have 100,000 downloads in a single month? Ensure your account for a reasonable quantity of sales and interest in your budgeting. Do you anticipate that marketing will bring in business? Keep in mind that advertising is usually ineffective, so you'll need to rely on other methods, such as word-of-mouth, to bring in clients.

## Know exactly what you're offering and how to sell it.

Your product must help people. Your own biases should not be included in the valuation. If you care about the company's success, it stands to reason that you think your products and services are worthwhile. You should seek outside advice to ensure the value is crystal apparent and simply articulated to your target audience. Imagine that a coworker of yours recommends your service to another coworker, stating something like, "You need to buy Service X since it will help you do A, provide you B, and offer insights into C." If the product's value cannot be clearly articulated, the company is doomed to fail. Getaroom.com offers great value because of the low prices and high quality of service it provides. When competition is fierce, as it often is in the hotel industry, differentiating factors such as low costs and excellent customer service may make a huge difference.

Niche companies that provide a compelling service may find a place to make money in growing markets with high total spending. Someone is constantly wanting to aid in travel research, keep tabs on it, or provide services for a certain kind or region of travel. The specialized service can generate revenue if it has a compelling selling point and a large enough customer base.

## Make sure your company concept is solid.

A company owner might have the most innovative product on the market that provides enormous value, but if his business strategy is flawed, he has nothing. An organization's success hinges on its "how": specifically, how it intends to advance its service while maintaining low overhead. How can you guarantee that your product will have a reasonable level of long-term demand? Explain how you will reach your target market while keeping costs down. Most companies fail, and it's not usually because of a bad concept. Of course, having a well-thought-out economic strategy in place is no guarantee of success, but it is essential and may help you use setbacks as learning opportunities rather than the precipitating factor in your financial demise.

Even with a good model in place, making adjustments or trying something new may be necessary. We implemented flash promotions, for instance, where customers only had a day or so to make a reservation. In order to encourage quick decision-making, we often discount these events by 10% to 60%. These deals aren't advertised in advance but appear when they're most likely to generate interest.

## Attract clients without breaking the bank.

Now that you have the goods or services and a strategy in place, you need to get people to buy them. As I said previously, commercials usually fail to achieve their intended results. Consider your social media approach and low-cost promos as strategies to draw in customers. You may spark discussions about your business and its products by soliciting reviews and facilitating user-generated material that highlights your product's benefits.

Although none of this may come as a huge surprise, I'm always surprised by how many startup founders fail to complete their research. Get these stipulations out of the way before you launch your company if you want to succeed despite the odds.

## Strategies for identifying and capitalizing on market opportunities

In the context of entrepreneurship, the key to success is learning how to spot and take advantage of openings in the market. A market opportunity exists when a need in the market is not currently being met. Entrepreneurs who want to capitalize on market possibilities should start by gathering information about their potential customers, their rivals, and the state of their industry as a whole via market research. Methods like questionnaires, focus groups, and electronic databases may be used to gather and analyze this kind of information. After a gap in the market has been recognized, business owners may begin formulating a plan to fill it. Creating a minimal viable product, testing it with prospective consumers for input, and iteratively improving the offering based on that data may all be part of this process. You may also take advantage of market openings by forming strategic alliances, promoting your business extensively online through content marketing and social media, and providing attractive discounts and specials to clients. Ultimately, it takes a blend of imagination, strategic planning, and familiarity with one's target audience's wants and requirements to spot and capitalize on market openings.

One of your most significant advantages as a corporation is the ability to spot and seize on promising new prospects. In that light, consider these pointers:

**Evaluate your environment:** What are your options, if any? It's worth noting that you can succeed in almost any setting if you're adaptable enough. Look at what's popular now and see if there are any ways you can adapt to meet the needs of your target audience. Where do we stand in terms of current events and information? Might your current offerings be modified to better handle these concerns?

**Evaluate self:** Knowing your company's strengths can help you take advantage of opportunities. That's what makes you unique and helps you succeed in business. People are more cautious with their money and want to know why they should spend money on your goods or services rather than the competition's during a recession or down markets. Therefore, they are extremely crucial.

**Align strengths with opportunities:** Get your ducks in a row by matching your talents to the possibilities available in the market. Suppose you own a bakery and see that more and more people are losing their jobs but that you also produce the greatest bespoke cakes in town. In that case, you might advertise how to make a loved one feel special when they find employment despite the challenging economic climate. You need to establish a perspective that works for your company and puts the spotlight on your strengths while downplaying any weaknesses.

**Shore up weaknesses:** When assessing your own performance, it is important to consider your areas of weakness. Is there a pattern of delays in your past shipments? Bad service to the public? Substandard components? Ask your customers where you can improve; they will tell you where you fall short. Instead of taking criticism personally, utilize it to grow and develop so that your flaws no longer result in missed opportunities.

**Be entrepreneurial minded:** This is the single most significant quality you can have. You may make money from the apocalypse hysteria by pre-selling post-apocalyptic services. Likewise, you might peddle food-prep supplies. Discover a technique to create a mobile app if people are particularly interested in your product or service on this platform. It is much simpler to capitalize on business chances if you think creatively and make the most of what's happening around you.

You need to be aware of your and your rivals' vulnerabilities and creative ways to reach out to clients and satisfy their wants and requirements. Being receptive to new ideas might help your company thrive at a time when traditional tactics are rapidly becoming irrelevant.

## Techniques for scaling and expanding your business over time

Expanding the company's bottom line is just part of what it takes to make it successful. The correct company strategy, staff, and procedures are essential while expanding to accommodate more clients and goods. Although it's every CEO's ambition to see their company explode suddenly, rapid growth requires planning for the long haul and sticking to it. No matter how big or little your company is, you need to know what it takes to expand to the next level.

Scale and growth are frequently used interchangeably but mean essentially the same thing. They are similar, but not the same thing at all. The term "growth" is used to describe the process through which a company's revenue grows at the same pace as it invests in expanding its human, technological, and financial assets. In contrast, scaling occurs when a business finds more effective means of expansion, leading to a rise in earnings that outpaces the cost of doing business by a wide margin.

**A few common blunders that companies make while expanding are:**

- Rapid expansion
- favoring the immediate above the permanent
- Having difficulty concentrating
- Hiring in bulk rather than carefully
- Putting efficiency at risk by ignoring procedures and systems
- Not very nimble

Successful businesses that expand their operations think about how the change will affect the whole company as they plan for it. Essential components consist of:

Aspirations of the firm. Setting both short-term and long-term goals is essential while aiming to expand your organisation. Putting too much emphasis on the here and now might cause your company to rush expansion at the expense of the foundation it needs to last.

Your approach for scaling up should take both your result and process objectives into account. You may think of outcome goals as the endpoint you're shooting for, and process objectives as the means by which you'll get there. To increase client retention by 100%, for instance, you'll need to devise a plan to boost customer satisfaction and involvement. Maintaining a flexible approach to goal-setting is also essential so that your team may adjust course quickly and effectively in response to changes in the market or in the demands of your customers.

Individuals included in a group. It's common for fast-growing companies to assume that doubling their workforce size is necessary to meet their sales goals. If sales growth rates flatten, this isn't a plan that will last. Focus on quality above number while assembling a team. Recruit capable managers to aid with team direction and morale. Recruit highly-skilled employees who can help you achieve your objectives.

Operation inside the body. Implementing efficient, standardised procedures and routines that can be repeated daily is crucial for developing a firm. Consider whether tasks, such as hiring new employees, billing clients, or requesting new marketing materials, may be automated or made more efficient to help your business expand.

Making up new procedures as team members finish tasks or put strategies into action is not a scalable method. More time is spent on physical labour, and it's harder to train new employees. Your company's capacity to expand will be greatly aided by the existence of well-documented procedures.

When you expand your company, keep these seven things in mind.

## Strategize how to increase sales

If you want to grow your company, increasing sales is the most important thing you can do. In order to increase sales, you may focus on either acquiring more customers or increasing the average revenue per customer. Both strategies are beneficial, but it is usually more cost-efficient to focus on deepening your connections with your present clientele. It might be six or seven times more expensive to acquire a new client than it is to maintain and expand relationships with existing ones.

To scale, as opposed to expand, your firm, you need to increase sales while increasing profits and decreasing costs.

**To boost sales, try using any of these best practises:**

- Concentrate on your intended audience.
- Learn about client habits and respond to comments by assembling a competent sales force
- Create a successful advertising strategy
- Relationship management (CRM) software allows you to manage your prospects and customers.
- Tweak your wording

## Invest in technology

According to worldwide research conducted by Automation Anywhere, the typical worker spends more than 40% of their time on mundane administrative duties that may be automated. Many of these jobs may be automated with the help of modern technology, allowing workers to devote their attention elsewhere, such as to the development of long-term plans and the achievement of strategic objectives.

You can get more out of the people you currently have working for you by automating routine chores.Investing in technologies that can automate operations like these may help your organisation grow.

- Induction of New Members
- Cash management and accounting
- Relationship management with clients
- Administration of a Project
- Establishing an Appointment

Consider the ease of use, customer support, timeliness of implementation, cost, and other factors when evaluating potential technology partners and providers as you plan to expand your organisation via automation.

Using technology to automate and standardize corporate operations is helpful when assembling a team. The process of scaling will go more smoothly if authorized technology is used and detailed instructions are documented for each jobs.

# Expand your team according to the market's needs

The first step in building the team you'll need to expand your firm is identifying the abilities you'll need to achieve your objectives and the areas in which your current staff may fall short.

The success of your firm depends on the hard and soft talents of your employees, so give some thought to them. Hard skills, often known as technical skills, are those that can be measured and applied directly to a certain occupation. The ability to work well with others, to set a good example, and to adopt a company's culture are all examples of soft talents. Soft talents are just as valuable as hard abilities but are more difficult to define and assess.

**Here are some examples of both hard and soft skills:**

Tough abilities. Skills in programming, business statistics, SEO, graphic design, and project management

The "soft" talents are essential. Soft skills: adaptability, communication, organization, time management, and service to customers

Think about your team's leaders, too, since they're the ones who have to set the tone and make sure everyone knows what they're supposed to be doing to reach the company's objectives.

The following are some examples of leadership abilities:

1. Receptive hearing Problem-solving Establishing rapport
2. Empathy and the ability to delegate
3. If you're looking for top-tier developers, designers, marketers, creatives, and other professionals on the Up work platform, look no further than Talent Scout

## Get external help

At the first phases of a company's development, its core team often consists of just a few people who are expected to fill a variety of roles. But, in the long term, it might be expensive to expect every team member to be a high-performing generalist. If you want to grow your company, one strategy to explore is hiring qualified professionals to help you streamline operations and increase productivity.

If full-time employees aren't yet required, it might be expensive and difficult to scale up to accommodate for their presence. Independent experts, however, provide a more cost-effective alternative, and they are being embraced by organizations worldwide. In fact, 78 percent of companies have utilized freelancers working remotely in the previous year, and 47 percent expect to increase their reliance on remote workers in the coming years.

Independent experts are typically brought in on an as-needed basis and paid on a per-project basis to avoid the hassle of putting up a business case and getting budget clearance for full-time employees. As a result, instead of paying a set wage to an employee, you may treat their salary as a variable expense. Scaling your staff in this way helps save money, increase output, and foster company flexibility.

If you're in need of highly skilled contractors to help you expand your company, you don't have to go about finding them on your own. Enterprise Suite is a robust system that provides quick access to the best freelance experts in any field. In order to swiftly cover internal talent shortages and develop your ideal team, Enterprise Suite removes all the logistical and operational burdens you would otherwise have to bear.

## Create a plan around realistic goal

Successfully expanding businesses know how to create objectives that are both achievable and stretch them. Demotivated employees might hinder your company's growth if your goals aren't specific enough or attainable. After the leaders have settled on a course of action, they should share it with the rest of the team so that everyone can become enthusiastic about contributing.

Let's assume you want to boost sales by 50% in the next year as an example. You may break this down into smaller, monthly or quarterly goals. Based on past data showing the typical number of meetings needed to complete a transaction, this information may be used to establish expectations for individual team members about the overall number of calls and meetings with prospects.

Take into account annual cycles while developing a strategy or timetable for accomplishing objectives. While numerous individuals are on vacation, business activity may decrease, such as sales or hiring. When breaking down your monthly or quarterly goals, have a strategy in place to accommodate for these slower times. It's a good idea to hire a professional business planner to help you create and implement a strategy that will allow your company to expand efficiently.

## Acquire Competent Management Abilities

Managers in your company are tasked with inspiring their teams to work towards individual objectives and holding them to account for the results they produce. The possibility of successful expansion of your business is directly related to the quality of its management team. So, it is essential that managers across all functional areas possess the appropriate competencies to propel the organisation towards its goals.

Determine which abilities will help your firm grow the greatest, and then seek to cultivate them among your present team members, recruit new employees, or bring in business managers.

**These are examples of management skills:**

- Mental deliberation
- Strategy making
- Managing one's time
- Managing transformation
- Leadership

## Focus the company's offerings

Businesses that priorities growth above size do all they can to increase their income, including appealing to a wider audience with a broader range of products and services. This strategy may boost short-term profits, but it usually comes with drawbacks that prevent it from being sustainable in the long run.

When a firm isn't laser-focused on what it offers, it risks attracting consumers who aren't a good match for its products or services, or it may lose sight of its existing clientele in favor of acquiring new ones. It also diminishes a company's ability to differentiate itself as a leader in a certain field or solution.

Successfully expanding businesses recognize the value of narrowing their emphasis to a certain niche market. This may put you ahead of the competition, help you better serve your core clients, and put you in a position to dominate your industry.

**Some suggestions for narrowing your business's focus:**

- Be aware of your own abilities and limitations.
- Find a specific market for your offerings (think customer size and industry)
- Determine the size of your potential customer base.
- Have a look at what the other guys are doing.
- Learn about the problems faced by your ideal clientele
- Observe the habits and likes of your present clientele for insight.
- Create products and content that alleviate client concerns.

Specializing your products and services is a great way to set yourself apart from the competition, but it's not a fix-all solution. If you want to grow your company over the long term, you need to adapt your products and services in response to changes in the market, emerging technologies, and your consumers' wants and requirements.

# Conclusion

One of your most significant advantages as a corporation is the ability to spot and seize on promising new prospects. In that light, consider these pointers:

Consider your surroundings. What are your options, if any? It's worth noting that you can succeed in almost any setting if you're adaptable enough. Look at what's popular now and see if there are any ways you can adapt to meet the needs of your target audience. Where do we stand in terms of current events and information? Might your current offerings be modified to better handle these concerns?

Review one's performance. Knowing your company's strengths can help you take advantage of opportunities. That's what makes you unique and helps you succeed in business. People are more cautious with their money and want to know why they should spend money on your goods or services rather than the competition's during a recession or down markets. Therefore, they are extremely crucial.

Get your ducks in a row by matching your talents to the possibilities available in the market. Suppose you own a bakery and see that more and more people are losing their jobs but that you also produce the greatest bespoke cakes in town. In that case, you might advertise how to make a loved one feel special when they find employment despite the challenging economic climate. You need to establish a perspective that works for your company and puts the spotlight on your strengths while downplaying any weaknesses.

Improve weak areas — When assessing your own performance, it is important to consider your areas of weakness. Is there a pattern of delays in your past shipments? Bad service to the public? Substandard components? Ask your customers where you can improve; they will tell you where you fall short. Instead of taking criticism personally, utilize it to grow and develop so that your flaws no longer result in missed opportunities. Think like an entrepreneur. This is the single most significant quality you can have. You may make money from the apocalypse hysteria by pre-selling post-apocalyptic services. Likewise, you might peddle food-prep supplies. Discover a technique to create a mobile app if people are particularly interested in your product or service on this platform. It is much simpler to capitalize on business chances if you think creatively and make the most of what's happening around you. we need to be aware of your and your rivals' vulnerabilities and creative ways to reach out to clients and satisfy their wants and requirements. Being receptive to new ideas might help your company thrive at a time when traditional tactics are rapidly becoming irrelevant.